CROCK·POT
· THE ORIGINAL SLOW COOKER ·

TABLE OF CONTENTS

SAVORY STARTERS 2
Appealing appetizers for snacking or entertaining

STEWS & CHILIES 18
Hearty soups to warm up cold nights

IMPRESS YOUR GUESTS 34
Fabulous fare that frees you up to join the party

EVERYDAY GOURMET 50
Make any day feel like a special occasion

WEEKNIGHT WINNERS 66
Easy to prepare family favorites

RECIPE INDEX 80

SAVORY STARTERS

Stuffed Baby Bell Peppers

- 1 tablespoon extra-virgin olive oil
- ½ medium onion, chopped
- ½ pound ground beef, chicken or turkey
- ½ cup cooked white rice
- 1 tablespoon dry dill weed
- 3 tablespoons fresh parsley, chopped
- 1 tablespoon tomato paste, divided
- 2 tablespoons lemon juice
- ⅛ teaspoon black pepper
- ½ teaspoon salt
- 1 bag yellow and red baby bell peppers (16 to 18 peppers)
- ¼ cup vegetable, chicken or beef broth

1. Heat oil in medium skillet over medium heat. Add onion and cook, stirring, 2 minutes or until onion is translucent. Add ground meat and cook, stirring, 8 to 10 minutes or until thoroughly browned. Transfer meat to bowl. Mix in rice, dill, parsley, ½ tablespoon tomato paste, lemon juice, pepper and salt. Mix well.

2. Using paring knife, make slit in side of each pepper and run under cold water to remove any small seeds. Spoon 2 to 3 teaspoons meat mixture into each pepper.

3. In **CROCK-POT®** slow cooker, whisk together broth and remaining ½ tablespoon tomato paste. Arrange peppers in broth, slit side up. Cover and cook on LOW 5 hours.

Makes 16 to 18 servings

Asian Barbecue Skewers

2 pounds boneless skinless chicken thighs

½ cup soy sauce

⅓ cup packed brown sugar

2 tablespoons sesame oil

3 cloves garlic, minced

½ cup thinly sliced green onions

1 tablespoon toasted sesame seeds (optional)

1. Cut each thigh into 4 pieces about 1½ inches thick. Thread chicken onto 7-inch-long wooden skewers, folding thinner pieces, if necessary. Place skewers in **CROCK-POT®** slow cooker, layering as flat as possible.

2. Combine soy sauce, brown sugar, oil and garlic in small bowl. Reserve ⅓ cup sauce; set aside. Pour remaining sauce over skewers. Cover; cook on LOW 2 hours. Turn skewers over and cook 1 hour longer.

3. Transfer skewers to serving platter. Discard cooking liquid. Spoon on reserved sauce and sprinkle with sliced green onions and sesame seeds, if desired.

Makes 4 to 6 servings

Chicken Croustade

2 tablespoons canola oil

1½ pounds boneless skinless chicken breasts, chopped into ¼-inch pieces

   Salt and black pepper

1 shallot, minced

¼ cup white wine

1 large portobello mushroom cap, chopped into ¼-inch pieces

1 tablespoon fresh thyme

¼ teaspoon sweet paprika

¼ teaspoon cumin

¼ cup chicken broth

1 package (6 shells) puff pastry shells or ½ package (1 sheet) puff pastry dough*

1 egg yolk

2 tablespoons cream

3 tablespoons freshly grated Parmesan cheese

   Minced chives, for garnish

If using puff pastry sheets, thaw, then slice each sheet into 9 squares; bake according to package directions.

1. Heat oil in large skillet over medium heat. Season chicken with salt and pepper and add to skillet. Brown chicken about 4 minutes; do not stir. Turn and brown other side. Place chicken in **CROCK-POT®** slow cooker.

2. Return skillet to low heat and add shallot. Cook 1 minute until shallot softens. Add white wine. Stir to scrape up any brown bits. Cook liquid down to 2 tablespoons then add shallot mixture to **CROCK-POT®** slow cooker. Stir in mushroom, thyme, paprika, cumin, broth, salt and pepper; mix well. Cover and cook on LOW 3 hours.

3. With 1 hour left in cooking time, bake pastry shells according to package directions.

4. With 20 minutes left in cooking time, beat egg yolk and cream together. Add 1 tablespoon cooking liquid from chicken, beating constantly. Whisk mixture into **CROCK-POT®** slow cooker. Cook uncovered on LOW remaining 20 minutes. Stir in Parmesan. Serve chicken filling over puff pastry; garnish with chives.

Makes 6 to 9 servings

Angel Wings

1 can (10¾ ounces) condensed tomato soup, undiluted

¾ cup water

¼ cup packed brown sugar

2½ tablespoons balsamic vinegar

2 tablespoons chopped shallots

10 chicken wings

1. Combine soup, water, brown sugar, vinegar and shallots in **CROCK-POT®** slow cooker; mix well.

2. Add chicken wings; stir to coat with sauce. Cover; cook on LOW 5 to 6 hours or until cooked through.

Makes 2 servings

Honey-Glazed Chicken Wings

3 tablespoons vegetable oil, divided

3 pounds chicken wings, tips removed

1 cup honey

½ cup soy sauce

1 clove garlic, minced

2 tablespoons tomato paste

2 teaspoons water

1 teaspoon sugar

1 teaspoon black pepper

1. Heat 1½ tablespoons oil in skillet over medium heat until hot. Brown chicken wings on each side in batches to prevent crowding. Turn each piece as it browns, about 1 to 2 minutes per side. Transfer with slotted spoon to **CROCK-POT®** slow cooker.

2. Combine honey, soy sauce, remaining 1½ tablespoons vegetable oil, and garlic in medium bowl. Whisk in tomato paste, water, sugar and pepper. Pour sauce over chicken. Cover; cook on LOW 6 to 8 hours or on HIGH 3 to 4 hours.

Makes 6 to 8 servings

Chicken and Asiago Stuffed Mushrooms

20 **large white mushrooms, stems removed and reserved**

3 **tablespoons extra-virgin olive oil, divided**

¼ **cup finely chopped onion**

2 **garlic cloves, minced**

¼ **cup Madeira wine**

½ **pound chicken sausage, removed from the casing, or ½ pound ground chicken**

1 **cup grated Asiago cheese**

½ **cup Italian seasoned bread crumbs**

3 **tablespoons chopped fresh parsley**

½ **teaspoon salt**

¼ **teaspoon black pepper**

1. Lightly brush mushrooms with 1 tablespoon oil and set aside. Finely chop mushroom stems.

2. Heat remaining 2 tablespoons oil in large nonstick skillet over medium-high heat. Add onion and cook until just beginning to soften, about 1 minute. Add chopped mushroom stems and cook until beginning to brown, 5 to 6 minutes. Stir in garlic and cook 1 minute. Pour in Madeira and cook until evaporated, about 1 minute. Add sausage and cook, stirring, until no longer pink, 3 to 4 minutes. Remove from heat and cool 5 minutes. Stir in cheese, bread crumbs, parsley, salt and pepper.

3. Divide mushroom mixture among mushroom caps, pressing slightly on filling to compress. Place stuffed mushrooms in **CROCK-POT®** slow cooker; cover and cook on HIGH 2 hours or until mushrooms are tender and filling is cooked through.

Makes 4 to 5 servings

Chicken Liver Pâté

1½ **pounds chicken livers, trimmed of fat and membrane**

1 **small onion, thinly sliced**

3 **sprigs fresh thyme**

2 **cloves garlic, peeled and lightly smashed**

¼ **teaspoon salt**

3 **tablespoons cold butter, cut into 4 pieces**

2 **tablespoons heavy cream**

2 **tablespoons sherry**

½ **shallot, minced**

2 **tablespoons fresh parsley, minced**

1 **tablespoon sherry vinegar**

⅛ **teaspoon sugar**

Salt and black pepper

Melba toast crackers or toast points, for serving

1. Rinse chicken livers and pat dry. Place in **CROCK-POT®** slow cooker. Add onion, thyme, garlic and ¼ teaspoon salt. Add 1 tablespoon water, cover and cook on LOW 1½ hours.

2. Remove thyme sprigs and discard. Place chicken liver mixture in food processor and pulse to create coarse paste. Add butter pieces one at a time, pulsing to combine. Add cream and sherry and pulse until combined. Transfer mixture to bowl to serve immediately, or place in a small loaf pan and cover with plastic wrap, pressing wrap directly against surface of pâté. Refrigerate overnight until set.

3. Mix shallot, parsley, vinegar, sugar, salt and pepper and let sit for 2 to 3 minutes. Spread on top of pâté. Serve with Melba crackers or toast points.

Makes 8 to 10 servings

Moroccan Spiced Chicken Wings

¼ cup orange juice

3 tablespoons tomato paste

2 teaspoons ground cumin

1 teaspoon curry powder

1 teaspoon ground turmeric

½ teaspoon ground cinnamon

½ teaspoon ground ginger

1 teaspoon salt

1 tablespoon olive oil

5 pounds chicken wings, tips removed and split at joint

In **CROCK-POT®** slow cooker, combine juice, tomato paste, cumin, curry, turmeric, cinnamon, ginger and salt. Heat oil in large nonstick skillet over medium-high heat. Add wings and brown in several batches, about 6 minutes per batch. Transfer wings to **CROCK-POT®** slow cooker. Toss well to coat with sauce. Cover and cook on HIGH 3 to 3½ hours or until tender.

Makes 8 servings

Oriental Chicken Wings

32 pieces chicken wing drums and flats

1 cup chopped red onion

1 cup soy sauce

¾ cup packed light brown sugar

¼ cup dry cooking sherry

2 tablespoons chopped fresh ginger

2 cloves garlic, minced

Chopped fresh chives (optional)

1. Preheat broiler. Broil chicken wing pieces about 5 minutes per side; transfer to **CROCK-POT®** slow cooker.

2. Combine onion, soy sauce, brown sugar, sherry, ginger and garlic in large bowl. Add to **CROCK-POT®** slow cooker; stir to blend well.

3. Cover and cook on LOW 5 to 6 hours or on HIGH 2 to 3 hours. Sprinkle with chives, if desired.

Makes 32 appetizers

Moroccan Spiced Chicken Wings

Cranberry-Barbecue Chicken Wings

3 pounds chicken wings

Salt and black pepper

1 jar (12 ounces) cranberry-orange relish

½ cup barbecue sauce

2 tablespoons quick-cooking tapioca

1 tablespoon prepared mustard

1. Preheat broiler. Cut off chicken wing tips; discard. Cut each wing in half at joint. Place chicken on rack in broiler pan; season with salt and pepper. Broil 4 to 5 inches from heat for 10 to 12 minutes or until browned, turning once. Transfer chicken to **CROCK-POT®** slow cooker.

2. Stir together relish, barbecue sauce, tapioca and mustard in small bowl. Pour over chicken. Cover; cook on LOW 4 to 5 hours.

Makes about 16 appetizer servings or 4 main dish servings

For a meal: *Serve one-fourth of wings with rice for a main dish.*

Asian Chicken "Fondue"

1 cup shiitake mushrooms, stems removed

2 cups chicken broth

1 tablespoon teriyaki sauce*

1 small leek, trimmed and chopped (both white and green parts)

1 head baby bok choy, trimmed and roughly chopped

1 tablespoon mirin (Japanese rice wine)*

2 tablespoons oyster sauce*

1 tablespoon canola oil

2 pounds boneless chicken breasts, cut into 1-inch cubes

Salt and black pepper

1 cup cubed butternut squash

1 can (8 ounces) baby corn, drained

1 can (8 ounces) water chestnuts, drained

1 tablespoon cornstarch

2 tablespoons cold water

Available in the Asian foods aisle of your local market.

1. In **CROCK-POT®** slow cooker, combine mushrooms, chicken broth, teriyaki sauce, leek, bok choy, mirin and oyster sauce.

2. Heat canola oil in skillet over medium heat. Season chicken with salt and pepper and add to skillet. Cook and stir until chicken is lightly browned on all sides. Transfer chicken to **CROCK-POT®** slow cooker. Add butternut squash. Cook on LOW 4½ to 5 hours.

3. With 20 minutes left in cooking time, add baby corn and water chestnuts. In small bowl, whisk together cornstarch and water to achieve consistency of heavy cream. Stir cornstarch mixture into **CROCK-POT®** slow cooker. Continue to cook, covered on LOW remaining 20 minutes.

4. Serve in **CROCK-POT®** slow cooker, set to WARM using bamboo skewers to spear meat and vegetables.

Makes 6 to 8 servings

Thai Coconut Chicken Meatballs

1 **pound ground chicken**

2 **green onions, chopped (both white and green parts)**

1 **clove garlic, minced**

2 **teaspoons toasted sesame oil**

1 **teaspoon fish sauce***

2 **teaspoons mirin (Japanese rice wine)***

1 **tablespoon canola oil**

½ **cup coconut milk**

¼ **cup chicken broth**

1 **teaspoon Thai red curry paste***

2 **teaspoons brown sugar**

2 **teaspoons lime juice**

1 **tablespoon cornstarch**

2 **tablespoons cold water**

Available in the Asian foods aisle of your local market.

1. In large bowl, combine chicken, green onions, garlic, sesame oil, fish sauce and mirin. Mix well with hands and form into 1½-inch meatballs.

2. Heat canola oil in skillet over medium heat. Add meatballs and cook, stirring until lightly browned. Alternatively, place meatballs on a cookie sheet and spray with cooking spray. Broil in oven until lightly browned.

3. Place meatballs in **CROCK-POT®** slow cooker. Add coconut milk, chicken broth, curry paste and sugar. Cover and cook on HIGH 3½ to 4 hours.

4. Add lime juice and mix well. In small bowl, whisk together cornstarch and cold water, stirring until it has consistency of heavy cream. Add to **CROCK-POT®** slow cooker. Cook, uncovered on HIGH 10 to 15 minutes longer or until sauce is thick enough to coat meatballs.

Makes 12 to 15 meatballs

STEWS & CHILIES

Black and White Chili

1 pound chicken tenders, cut into ¾-inch pieces

1 cup coarsely chopped onion

1 can (about 15 ounces) Great Northern beans, drained

1 can (about 15 ounces) black beans, drained

1 can (about 14 ounces) Mexican-style stewed tomatoes, undrained

2 tablespoons Texas-style chili powder seasoning mix

1. Spray large skillet with cooking spray; heat over medium heat until hot. Add chicken and onion; cook and stir 5 minutes or until chicken is browned.

2. Combine chicken mixture, beans, tomatoes with juice and chili seasoning in **CROCK-POT®** slow cooker. Cover; cook on LOW 4 to 4½ hours.

Makes 6 servings

Serving Suggestion: *For a change of pace, this delicious chili is excellent served over cooked rice or pasta.*

Chinese Chicken Stew

1 pound boneless skinless chicken thighs, cut into 1-inch pieces

1 teaspoon Chinese five-spice powder*

½ to ¾ teaspoon red pepper flakes

1 tablespoon peanut or vegetable oil

1 large onion, coarsely chopped

1 package (8 ounces) fresh mushrooms, sliced

2 cloves garlic, minced

1 can (about 14 ounces) chicken broth, divided

1 tablespoon cornstarch

1 large red bell pepper, cut into ¾-inch pieces

2 tablespoons soy sauce

2 large green onions, cut into ½-inch pieces

1 tablespoon sesame oil

3 cups hot cooked white rice (optional)

¼ cup coarsely chopped fresh cilantro (optional)

*Chinese five-spice powder is a blend of cinnamon, cloves, fennel seed, anise and Szechuan peppercorns. It is available in most supermarkets and at Asian grocery stores.

1. Toss chicken with five-spice powder and red pepper flakes in small bowl. Heat peanut oil in large skillet. Add onion and chicken; cook and stir about 5 minutes or until chicken is browned. Add mushrooms and garlic; cook and stir until chicken is no longer pink.

2. Combine ¼ cup broth and cornstarch in small bowl; set aside. Place cooked chicken mixture, remaining broth, bell pepper and soy sauce in **CROCK-POT®** slow cooker. Cover; cook on LOW 3½ hours or until peppers are tender.

3. Stir in cornstarch mixture, green onions and sesame oil. Cook 30 to 45 minutes or until thickened. Ladle into soup bowls; scoop ½ cup rice into each bowl and sprinkle with cilantro, if desired.

Makes 6 servings (about 5 cups)

Greek-Style Chicken Stew

2 cups sliced mushrooms

2 cups cubed peeled eggplant

1¼ cups reduced-sodium chicken broth

¾ cup coarsely chopped onion

2 cloves garlic, minced

1½ teaspoons all-purpose flour

1 teaspoon dried oregano

½ teaspoon dried basil

½ teaspoon dried thyme

6 skinless chicken breasts, about 2 pounds

Additional all-purpose flour

3 tablespoons dry sherry or reduced-sodium chicken broth

¼ teaspoon salt

¼ teaspoon black pepper

1 can (14 ounces) artichoke hearts, drained

12 ounces uncooked wide egg noodles

1. Combine mushrooms, eggplant, broth, onion, garlic, flour, oregano, basil and thyme in **CROCK-POT®** slow cooker. Cover; cook on HIGH 1 hour.

2. Coat chicken very lightly with flour. Generously spray large nonstick skillet with cooking spray; heat over medium heat until hot. Cook chicken 10 to 15 minutes or until browned on all sides.

3. Remove vegetables to bowl with slotted spoon. Layer chicken in **CROCK-POT®** slow cooker; return vegetables to **CROCK-POT®** slow cooker. Add sherry, salt and pepper. Reduce heat to LOW. Cover; cook 6 to 6½ hours or until chicken is no longer pink in center and vegetables are tender.

4. Stir in artichokes; cover and cook 45 minutes to 1 hour or until heated through. Cook noodles according to package directions. Serve chicken stew over noodles.

Makes 6 servings

Chicken Stew
with Herb Dumplings

2 cans (about 14 ounces each) chicken broth, divided

2 cups sliced carrots

1 cup chopped onion

1 large green bell pepper, sliced

½ cup sliced celery

⅔ cup all-purpose flour

1 pound boneless skinless chicken breasts, cut into 1-inch pieces

1 large potato, unpeeled and cut into 1-inch pieces

6 ounces mushrooms, halved

¾ cup frozen peas

1 teaspoon dried basil

¾ teaspoon dried rosemary

¼ teaspoon dried tarragon

¾ to 1 teaspoon salt

¼ teaspoon black pepper

¼ cup whipping cream

Herb Dumplings

1 cup biscuit baking mix

¼ teaspoon dried basil

¼ teaspoon dried rosemary

⅛ teaspoon dried tarragon

⅓ cup milk

1. Reserve 1 cup chicken broth. Combine carrots, onion, bell pepper, celery and remaining chicken broth in **CROCK-POT®** slow cooker. Cover; cook on LOW 2 hours.

2. Stir remaining 1 cup broth into flour until smooth. Stir into **CROCK-POT®** slow cooker. Add chicken, potato, mushrooms, peas, 1 teaspoon basil, ¾ teaspoon rosemary and ¼ teaspoon tarragon to **CROCK-POT®** slow cooker. Cover; cook 4 hours or until vegetables are tender and chicken is tender. Stir in salt, black pepper and cream.

3. Combine baking mix, ¼ teaspoon basil, ¼ teaspoon rosemary and ⅛ teaspoon tarragon in small bowl. Stir in milk to form soft dough. Spoon dumpling mixture on top of stew in 4 large spoonfuls. Cook, uncovered, 30 minutes. Cover; cook 30 to 45 minutes or until dumplings are firm and toothpick inserted in centers comes out clean. Serve in shallow bowls.

Makes 4 servings

Chipotle Chicken Stew

1 **pound boneless skinless chicken thighs, cut into cubes**

1 **can (15 ounces) navy beans, drained and rinsed**

1 **can (15 ounces) black beans, drained and rinsed**

1 **can (14½ ounces) crushed tomatoes, undrained**

1½ **cups chicken broth**

½ **cup orange juice**

1 **medium onion, diced**

1 **chipotle pepper in adobo sauce, minced**

1 **teaspoon salt**

1 **teaspoon ground cumin**

1 **bay leaf**

Cilantro sprigs (optional)

1. Combine chicken, beans, tomatoes with juice, broth, orange juice, onion, chipotle pepper, salt, cumin and bay leaf in **CROCK-POT®** slow cooker.

2. Cover; cook on LOW 7 to 8 hours or on HIGH 3½ to 4 hours. Remove bay leaf before serving. Garnish with cilantro sprigs, if desired.

Makes 6 servings

Quatro Frijoles con Pollo Cantaro

1 cup pitted black olives, drained

1 pound boneless skinless chicken breasts, cubed*

1 can (16 ounces) garbanzo beans, drained and rinsed

1 can (16 ounces) Great Northern or navy beans, drained and rinsed

1 can (15 ounces) cannellini beans, drained and rinsed

1 can (16 ounces) red kidney beans, drained and rinsed

1 can (7 ounces) chopped mild green chiles, drained

2 cups chicken stock, plus extra as needed

2 tablespoons canola or olive oil

1 cup minced onion

2 teaspoons minced garlic

1½ teaspoons ground cumin

Hot sauce, to taste

Salt and black pepper, to taste

2 cups crushed corn chips

6 ounces Monterey Jack cheese, grated

Turkey, pork or beef can be substituted for chicken.

1. Combine olives, chicken, beans, chiles and chicken stock in **CROCK-POT®** slow cooker. Mix well; set aside.

2. Heat oil in large skillet over medium-high heat. Cook onion, garlic and cumin until onions are soft, stirring frequently. Add to chicken mixture. Cover; cook on LOW 4 to 5 hours. Check liquid about halfway through, adding more hot broth as needed.

3. Taste and add hot sauce, salt and pepper. Serve in warm bowls and garnish with corn chips and cheese.

Makes 6 servings

Chicken and Chile Pepper Stew

1 **pound boneless skinless chicken thighs, cut into ½-inch pieces**

1 **pound small potatoes, cut lengthwise into halves, then crosswise into slices**

1 **cup chopped onion**

2 **poblano chile peppers, seeded and cut into ½-inch pieces***

1 **jalapeño pepper, seeded and finely chopped***

3 **cloves garlic, minced**

3 **cups fat-free reduced-sodium chicken broth**

1 **can (about 14 ounces) no-salt-added diced tomatoes**

2 **tablespoons chili powder**

1 **teaspoon dried oregano**

Chile peppers can sting and irritate the skin, so wear rubber gloves when handling peppers and do not touch your eyes.

1. Place chicken, potatoes, onion, poblano peppers, jalapeño pepper and garlic in **CROCK-POT®** slow cooker.

2. Stir together broth, tomatoes, chili powder and oregano in large bowl. Pour broth mixture over chicken mixture in **CROCK-POT®** slow cooker; mix well. Cover; cook on LOW 8 to 9 hours.

Makes 6 servings

Chicken and Vegetable Chowder

1 **pound boneless skinless chicken breasts, cut into 1-inch pieces**

1 **can (about 14 ounces) reduced-sodium chicken broth**

1 **can (10¾ ounces) condensed cream of potato soup, undiluted**

1 **package (10 ounces) frozen broccoli florets, thawed**

1 **cup sliced carrots**

1 **jar (4½ ounces) sliced mushrooms, drained**

½ **cup chopped onion**

½ **cup whole kernel corn**

2 **cloves garlic, minced**

½ **teaspoon dried thyme leaves**

⅓ **cup half-and-half**

1. Combine chicken, broth, soup, broccoli, carrots, mushrooms, onion, corn, garlic and thyme in **CROCK-POT®** slow cooker; mix well. Cover; cook on LOW 5 to 6 hours.

2. Stir in half-and-half. Cover; cook on HIGH 15 minutes or until heated through.

Makes 6 servings

Variation: *Add ½ cup (2 ounces) shredded Swiss or Cheddar cheese just before serving, stirring over LOW heat until melted.*

Chicken and Sweet Potato Stew

4 boneless skinless chicken breasts, cut into bite-size pieces

2 medium sweet potatoes, peeled and cubed

2 medium Yukon Gold potatoes, peeled and cubed

2 medium carrots, peeled and cut into ½-inch slices

1 can (28 ounces) whole stewed tomatoes

1 teaspoon salt

1 teaspoon paprika

1 teaspoon celery seeds

½ teaspoon freshly ground black pepper

⅛ teaspoon ground cinnamon

⅛ teaspoon ground nutmeg

1 cup nonfat, low-sodium chicken broth

¼ cup fresh basil, chopped

1. Combine chicken, potatoes, carrots, tomatoes, salt, paprika, celery seeds, pepper, cinnamon, nutmeg and broth in **CROCK-POT®** slow cooker.

2. Cover; cook on LOW for 6 to 8 hours or on HIGH for 3 to 4 hours.

3. Sprinkle with basil just before serving.

Makes 6 servings

Note: *This light stew has an Indian influence and offers excellent flavor without the fat.*

Chicken and Black Bean Chili

1 pound boneless skinless chicken thighs, cut into 1-inch chunks

2 teaspoons chili powder

2 teaspoons ground cumin

¾ teaspoon salt

1 green bell pepper, diced

1 small onion, chopped

3 cloves garlic, minced

1 can (about 14 ounces) diced tomatoes, undrained

1 cup chunky salsa

1 can (about 15 ounces) black beans, drained and rinsed

Optional toppings: sour cream, diced ripe avocado, shredded Cheddar cheese, sliced green onions or chopped cilantro and/or crushed tortilla or corn chips (optional)

1. Combine chicken, chili powder, cumin and salt in **CROCK-POT®** slow cooker; toss to coat.

2. Add bell pepper, onion and garlic; mix well. Stir in tomatoes and salsa. Cover; cook on LOW 5 to 6 hours or on HIGH 2½ to 3 hours or until chicken is tender.

3. Increase heat to HIGH; stir in beans. Cover; cook 5 to 10 minutes or until beans are heated through. Ladle into bowls; serve with desired toppings.

Makes 4 servings

Chicken Tangier

- 2 tablespoons dried oregano
- 2 teaspoons seasoning salt
- 2 teaspoons puréed garlic
- ¼ teaspoon black pepper
- 3 pounds skinless chicken thighs
- 8 thin slices lemon
- ½ cup dry white wine
- 2 tablespoons olive oil
- 1 cup pitted prunes
- ¼ cup currants or raisins
- ½ cup pitted green olives
- 2 tablespoons capers

  Hot cooked noodles or rice

  Chopped fresh parsley or cilantro, to garnish

1. Stir together oregano, salt, garlic and pepper in small bowl. Rub mixture onto chicken, coating on all sides.

2. Spray inside of **CROCK-POT®** slow cooker with cooking spray and add chicken. Tuck lemon slices between chicken pieces. Pour wine over chicken and sprinkle olive oil on top. Add prunes, currants, olives and capers. Cover and cook on LOW 7 to 8 hours or on HIGH 4 to 5 hours.

3. To serve, spoon over cooked noodles or rice and sprinkle with chopped fresh parsley or cilantro.

Makes 8 servings

Stuffed Chicken Breasts

6 **boneless skinless chicken breasts**

8 **ounces feta cheese, crumbled**

3 **cups chopped fresh spinach leaves**

⅓ **cup oil-packed sun-dried tomatoes, drained and chopped**

1 **teaspoon minced lemon peel**

1 **teaspoon dried basil, oregano or mint**

½ **teaspoon garlic powder**

Freshly ground black pepper, to taste

1 **can (15 ounces) diced tomatoes, undrained**

½ **cup oil-cured olives***

Hot cooked polenta

If using pitted olives, add to CROCK-POT® slow cooker in the final hour of cooking.

1. Place 1 chicken breast between 2 pieces of plastic wrap. Using tenderizer mallet or back of skillet, pound breast until about ¼-inch thick. Repeat with remaining chicken.

2. Combine feta, spinach, sun-dried tomatoes, lemon peel, basil, garlic powder and pepper in medium bowl.

3. Lay pounded chicken, smooth side down, on work surface. Place about 2 tablespoons feta mixture on wide end of breast. Roll tightly. Repeat with remaining chicken.

4. Place rolled chicken, seam side down, in **CROCK-POT®** slow cooker. Top with diced tomatoes with juice and olives. Cover; cook on LOW 5½ to 6 hours or on HIGH 4 hours. Serve with polenta.

Makes 6 servings

Forty-Clove Chicken

1 cut-up whole chicken (about 3 pounds)

Salt and black pepper

1 to 2 tablespoons olive oil

¼ cup dry white wine

2 tablespoons chopped fresh parsley or 2 teaspoons dried parsley flakes

2 tablespoons dry vermouth

2 teaspoons dried basil

1 teaspoon dried oregano

Pinch red pepper flakes

40 cloves garlic (about 2 heads), peeled*

4 stalks celery, sliced

Juice and peel of 1 lemon

Fresh herbs

The whole garlic bulb is called a head.

1. Remove skin from chicken. Sprinkle chicken with salt and pepper. Heat oil in large skillet over medium heat. Add chicken; brown on all sides. Remove to platter.

2. Combine wine, parsley, vermouth, basil, oregano and red pepper flakes in large bowl. Add garlic and celery; coat well. Transfer garlic and celery to **CROCK-POT®** slow cooker with slotted spoon. Add chicken to remaining herb mixture; coat well. Place chicken on top of celery mixture in **CROCK-POT®** slow cooker. Sprinkle lemon juice and peel over chicken. Cover; cook on LOW 6 hours.

3. Sprinkle with fresh herbs before serving.

Makes 4 to 6 servings

Bistro Chicken in Rich Cream Sauce

- **4 skinless bone-in chicken breast halves, rinsed and patted dry (about 3 pounds total)**
- **½ cup dry white wine, divided**
- **1 tablespoon or ½ packet (0.7 ounces) Italian salad dressing and seasoning mix**
- **½ teaspoon dried oregano**
- **1 can (10¾ ounces) condensed cream of chicken soup, undiluted**
- **3 ounces cream cheese, cut into cubes**
- **¼ teaspoon salt**
- **⅛ teaspoon black pepper**
- **2 tablespoons chopped fresh parsley**

1. Coat **CROCK-POT®** slow cooker with nonstick cooking spray. Arrange chicken in single layer in bottom, overlapping slightly. Pour ¼ cup wine over chicken. Sprinkle evenly with salad dressing mix and oregano. Cover; cook on LOW 5 to 6 hours or on HIGH 3 hours.

2. Transfer chicken to plate with slotted spoon. Turn **CROCK-POT®** slow cooker to HIGH. Whisk soup, cream cheese, salt and pepper into cooking liquid. (Mixture will be a bit lumpy.) Arrange chicken on top. Cover; cook 15 to 20 minutes longer to heat through.

3. Transfer chicken to shallow pasta bowl. Add remaining ¼ cup wine to sauce and whisk until smooth. To serve, spoon sauce around chicken, and garnish with parsley.

Makes 4 servings

Indian-Style Apricot Chicken

6 **chicken thighs, rinsed and patted dry**

¼ **teaspoon salt**

¼ **teaspoon black pepper**

1 **tablespoon vegetable oil**

1 **large onion, chopped**

2 **cloves garlic, minced**

2 **tablespoons grated fresh ginger**

½ **teaspoon ground cinnamon**

⅛ **teaspoon ground allspice**

1 **can (14½ ounces) diced tomatoes, undrained**

1 **cup chicken broth**

1 **package (8 ounces) dried apricots**

1 **pinch saffron threads (optional)**

Hot basmati rice

2 **tablespoons chopped fresh parsley**

1. Coat **CROCK-POT®** slow cooker with nonstick cooking spray. Season chicken with salt and pepper. Heat oil in large skillet over medium-high heat until hot. Brown chicken on all sides. Transfer to **CROCK-POT®** slow cooker.

2. Add onion to skillet. Cook and stir 3 to 5 minutes or until translucent. Stir in garlic, ginger, cinnamon and allspice. Cook and stir 15 to 30 seconds longer or until mixture is fragrant. Add tomatoes with juice and broth. Cook 2 to 3 minutes or until mixture is heated through. Pour into **CROCK-POT®** slow cooker.

3. Add apricots and saffron, if desired. Cover; cook on LOW 5 to 6 hours or on HIGH 3 to 3½ hours or until chicken is tender. Add salt and pepper, if desired. Serve with basmati rice and garnish with chopped parsley.

Makes 4 to 6 servings

Note: *Use skinless chicken thighs, if desired. To skin chicken easily, grasp skin with paper towel and pull away. Repeat with fresh paper towel for each piece of chicken, discarding skins and towels.*

Coq au Vin

2 cups frozen pearl onions, thawed

4 slices thick-cut bacon, crisp-cooked and crumbled

1 cup sliced button mushrooms

1 clove garlic, minced

1 teaspoon dried thyme

⅛ teaspoon black pepper

6 boneless skinless chicken breasts (about 2 pounds)

½ cup dry red wine

¾ cup reduced-sodium chicken broth

¼ cup tomato paste

3 tablespoons all-purpose flour

Hot cooked egg noodles (optional)

1. Layer onions, bacon, mushrooms, garlic, thyme, pepper, chicken, wine and broth in **CROCK-POT®** slow cooker.

2. Cover; cook on LOW 6 to 8 hours.

3. Remove chicken and vegetables; cover and keep warm. Ladle ½ cup cooking liquid into small bowl; cool slightly. Mix reserved liquid, tomato paste and flour until smooth; stir into **CROCK-POT®** slow cooker. Cook; uncovered, on HIGH 15 minutes or until thickened. Serve over hot noodles, if desired.

Makes 6 servings

Cook's Nook: *Coq au Vin is a classic French dish that is made with bone-in chicken, salt pork or bacon, brandy, red wine and herbs. The dish originated when farmers needed a way to cook old chickens that could no longer breed. A slow, moist cooking method was needed to tenderize the tough old birds.*

Chicken Parmesan with Eggplant

6 boneless skinless chicken breasts

2 eggs

2 teaspoons salt

2 teaspoons black pepper

2 cups Italian bread crumbs

½ cup olive oil

½ cup (1 stick) butter

2 small eggplants, cut into ¾-inch-thick slices

1½ cups grated Parmesan cheese, divided

2½ cups tomato-basil sauce, divided

1 pound sliced or shredded mozzarella cheese

1. Slice chicken breasts in half lengthwise. Cut each half lengthwise again to get 4 (¾-inch) slices.

2. Combine eggs, salt and pepper in medium bowl. Place bread crumbs in separate bowl or on plate. Dip each chicken piece in egg, then coat in bread crumbs.

3. Heat oil and butter in skillet over medium heat until hot. Brown breaded chicken on all sides, turning as pieces brown. Transfer to paper-towel-lined plate to drain excess oil.

4. Layer eggplant on bottom of **CROCK-POT®** slow cooker. Add ¾ cup Parmesan cheese and 1¼ cups sauce. Arrange chicken on sauce. Add remaining Parmesan cheese and sauce. Top with mozzarella cheese. Cover; cook on LOW 6 hours or on HIGH 2 to 4 hours.

Makes 6 to 8 servings

Greek Chicken and Orzo

2 medium green bell peppers, cut into thin strips

1 cup chopped onion

2 teaspoons extra-virgin olive oil

8 skinless chicken thighs, rinsed and patted dry

1 tablespoon dried oregano

½ teaspoon dried rosemary

½ teaspoon garlic powder

¾ teaspoon salt, divided

⅜ teaspoon black pepper, divided

8 ounces uncooked dry orzo pasta

Juice and grated peel of 1 medium lemon

½ cup water

2 ounces crumbled feta cheese (optional)

Chopped fresh parsley (optional)

1. Coat **CROCK-POT®** slow cooker with nonstick cooking spray. Add bell peppers and onion.

2. Heat oil in large skillet over medium-high heat until hot. Brown chicken on both sides. Transfer to **CROCK-POT®** slow cooker, overlapping slightly if necessary. Sprinkle chicken with oregano, rosemary, garlic powder, ¼ teaspoon salt and ⅛ teaspoon black pepper. Cover; cook on LOW 5 to 6 hours or on HIGH 3 hours.

3. Transfer chicken to separate plate. Turn **CROCK-POT®** slow cooker to HIGH. Stir orzo, lemon juice, lemon peel, water and remaining ½ teaspoon salt and ¼ teaspoon black pepper into **CROCK-POT®** slow cooker. Top with chicken. Cover; cook on HIGH 30 minutes or until pasta is done. Garnish with feta cheese and parsley, if desired.

Makes 4 servings

Note: *To skin chicken easily, grasp skin with paper towel and pull away. Repeat with fresh paper towel for each piece of chicken, discarding skins and towels.*

Basque Chicken with Peppers

1 whole chicken (about 4 pounds), cut into 8 pieces

Salt and black pepper

1½ tablespoons olive oil

1 onion, chopped

1 medium green bell pepper, sliced

1 medium yellow bell pepper, sliced

1 medium red bell pepper, sliced

1 package (8 ounces) button or cremini mushrooms, halved

2 large cloves garlic, minced

½ cup Rioja wine

1 can (14½ ounces) stewed tomatoes, drained

3 tablespoons tomato paste

½ cup chicken stock

1 sprig marjoram

1 teaspoon smoked paprika

4 ounces diced prosciutto

1. Rinse chicken and pat dry. Season with salt and pepper. Heat olive oil in large skillet over medium-high heat. Add chicken pieces in batches and brown well on all sides. Transfer chicken to **CROCK-POT®** slow cooker.

2. When all chicken has been browned, reduce heat under skillet and add onion. Cook and stir 3 minutes or until softened. Add bell peppers and mushrooms; cook and stir 3 minutes. Stir in garlic, wine, tomatoes, tomato paste, chicken stock, marjoram and paprika. Season to taste with salt and pepper. Bring to simmer; simmer 3 to 4 minutes. Pour mixture over chicken in **CROCK-POT®** slow cooker. Cover and cook on HIGH 4 hours or until chicken is tender.

3. Remove chicken to deep platter or serving bowl with tongs. Spoon vegetables and sauce over chicken. Sprinkle with prosciutto and serve.

Makes 4 to 6 servings

CROCK·POT
· THE ORIGINAL SLOW COOKER ·

EVERYDAY GOURMET

Thai Chicken

2½ pounds chicken pieces

1 cup hot salsa

¼ cup peanut butter

2 tablespoons lime juice

1 tablespoon soy sauce

1 teaspoon minced fresh ginger

Cooked white rice, for serving

½ cup peanuts, chopped

2 tablespoons chopped fresh cilantro

1. Place chicken in **CROCK-POT®** slow cooker. In a bowl, mix together salsa, peanut butter, lime juice, soy sauce and ginger. Pour over chicken.

2. Cover; cook on LOW 8 to 9 hours or on HIGH 3 to 4 hours or until done.

3. To serve, place chicken over rice, pour sauce over chicken; sprinkle with peanuts and cilantro.

Makes 6 servings

Cerveza Chicken Enchilada Casserole

2 cups water

1 stalk celery, chopped

1 small carrot, peeled and chopped

1 bottle (12 ounces) Mexican beer, divided

   Juice of 1 lime

1 teaspoon salt

1½ pounds boneless skinless chicken breasts

1 can (19 ounces) enchilada sauce, divided

7 ounces white corn tortilla chips

½ medium onion, chopped

3 cups shredded Cheddar cheese

   Sour cream, sliced olives and cilantro (optional)

1. Heat water, celery, carrot, 1 cup beer, lime juice and salt in saucepan over high heat until boiling. Add chicken breasts; reduce heat to simmer. Cook until chicken is cooked through, about 12 to 14 minutes. Remove; cool and shred into bite-sized pieces.

2. Spoon ½ cup enchilada sauce in bottom of **CROCK-POT®** slow cooker. Place tortilla chips in 1 layer over sauce. Cover with ⅓ shredded chicken. Sprinkle ⅓ chopped onion over chicken. Add 1 cup cheese, spreading evenly. Pour ½ cup enchilada sauce over cheese. Repeat layering process 2 more times, pouring remaining beer over casserole before adding last layer of cheese.

3. Cook on LOW 3½ to 4 hours. Garnish with sour cream, sliced olives and cilantro, if desired.

Makes 4 to 6 servings

Mediterranean Chicken Breasts and Wild Rice

1 pound boneless skinless chicken breasts, lightly pounded

Kosher salt, to taste

Black pepper, to taste

1 cup white and wild rice blend

10 cloves garlic, smashed

½ cup oil-packed or dry sun-dried tomatoes*

½ cup capers, drained

2 cups water

½ cup fresh-squeezed lemon juice

¼ cup extra-virgin olive oil

If using dry sun-dried tomatoes, soak in boiling water to soften before chopping.

1. Season chicken with salt and black pepper. Place in **CROCK-POT®** slow cooker. Add rice, garlic, tomatoes and capers; stir well.

2. Mix water, lemon juice and oil in small mixing bowl. Pour mixture over rice and chicken. Stir once to coat chicken. Cover; cook on LOW 8 hours.

Makes 4 servings

Dijon Chicken Thighs with Artichoke Sauce

⅓ cup Dijon mustard

2 tablespoons chopped garlic

½ teaspoon dried tarragon

2½ pounds chicken thighs (about 8), skinned

1 cup chopped onion

1 cup sliced mushrooms

1 jar (12 ounces) quartered marinated artichoke hearts, undrained

¼ cup chopped fresh parsley

1. Combine mustard, garlic and tarragon in large bowl. Add chicken thighs and toss to coat. Transfer to **CROCK-POT®** slow cooker.

2. Add onion, mushrooms and artichokes with liquid. Cover; cook on LOW 6 to 8 hours or on HIGH 4 hours or until chicken is tender. Stir in parsley just before serving.

Makes 8 servings

Serving suggestion: *Serve with hot fettuccine that has been tossed with butter and parsley.*

Note: *To skin chicken easily, grasp skin with paper towel and pull away. Repeat with fresh paper towel for each piece of chicken, discarding skins and towels.*

Chipotle Chicken Casserole

1 pound boneless skinless chicken thighs, cut into cubes

1 teaspoon salt

1 teaspoon ground cumin

1 bay leaf

1 chipotle pepper in adobo sauce, minced

1 medium onion, diced

1 can (15 ounces) navy beans, drained and rinsed

1 can (15 ounces) black beans, drained and rinsed

1 can (14½ ounces) crushed tomatoes, undrained

1½ cups chicken broth

½ cup orange juice

¼ cup chopped fresh cilantro, for garnish (optional)

Combine chicken, salt, cumin, bay leaf, chipotle pepper, onion, beans, tomatoes with juice, broth and orange juice in **CROCK-POT®** slow cooker. Cover; cook on LOW 7 to 8 hours or on HIGH 3½ to 4 hours. Remove bay leaf before serving. Garnish with cilantro, if desired.

Makes 6 servings

Autumn Chicken

1 can (14 ounces) whole artichoke hearts, drained

1 can (14 ounces) whole mushrooms, divided

12 boneless skinless chicken breasts

1 jar (6½ ounces) marinated artichoke hearts, with liquid

¾ cup white wine

½ cup balsamic vinaigrette

Hot cooked noodles

Paprika, for garnish (optional)

Spread whole artichokes over bottom of **CROCK-POT®** slow cooker. Top with half the mushrooms. Layer chicken over mushrooms. Add marinated artichoke hearts with liquid. Add remaining mushrooms. Pour in wine and vinaigrette. Cover; cook on LOW 4 to 5 hours. Serve over noodles. Garnish with paprika, if desired.

Makes 10 to 12 servings

Chicken & Rice

3 cans (10¾ ounces each) condensed cream of chicken soup, undiluted

2 cups uncooked instant rice

1 cup water

1 pound boneless skinless chicken breasts or chicken breast tenders

½ teaspoon salt

¼ teaspoon paprika

¼ teaspoon black pepper

½ cup diced celery

Combine soup, rice and water in **CROCK-POT®** slow cooker. Add chicken; sprinkle with salt, paprika and pepper. Sprinkle celery over chicken. Cover; cook on LOW 6 to 8 hours or on HIGH 3 to 4 hours.

Makes 4 servings

Autumn Chicken

Chicken in Honey Sauce

4 to 6 boneless skinless chicken breasts

Salt

Black pepper

2 cups honey

1 cup soy sauce

½ cup ketchup

¼ cup oil

2 cloves garlic, minced

Sesame seeds

1. Place chicken in **CROCK-POT®** slow cooker; season with salt and pepper.

2. Combine honey, soy sauce, ketchup, oil and garlic in medium bowl. Pour over chicken. Cover; cook on LOW 6 to 8 hours or on HIGH 3 to 4 hours.

3. Garnish with sesame seeds before serving.

Makes 4 to 6 servings

Chicken Teriyaki

1 pound boneless skinless chicken tenders

1 can (6 ounces) pineapple juice

¼ cup soy sauce

1 tablespoon sugar

1 tablespoon minced fresh ginger

1 tablespoon minced garlic

1 tablespoon vegetable oil

1 tablespoon molasses

24 cherry tomatoes (optional)

2 cups hot cooked rice

Combine all ingredients except rice in **CROCK-POT®** slow cooker. Cover; cook on LOW 2 hours or until chicken is tender. Serve chicken and sauce over rice.

Makes 4 servings

Chicken in Honey Sauce

Provençal Lemon and Olive Chicken

2 **cups chopped onion**

8 **skinless chicken thighs (about 2½ pounds)**

1 **lemon, thinly sliced and seeds removed**

1 **cup pitted green olives**

1 **tablespoon olive brine from jar or 1 tablespoon white vinegar**

2 **teaspoons herbes de Provence**

1 **bay leaf**

½ **teaspoon salt**

⅛ **teaspoon black pepper**

1 **cup chicken broth**

½ **cup minced fresh parsley**

1. Place onion in **CROCK-POT®** slow cooker. Arrange chicken thighs over onion. Place lemon slice on each thigh. Add olives, brine, herbes de Provence, bay leaf, salt and pepper. Slowly pour in chicken broth.

2. Cover; cook on LOW 5 to 6 hours or on HIGH 3 to 3½ hours or until chicken is tender. Stir in parsley before serving.

Makes 8 servings

Note: *To skin chicken easily, grasp skin with paper towel and pull away. Repeat with fresh paper towel for each piece of chicken, discarding skins and towels.*

Cashew Chicken

6 boneless skinless chicken breasts

1½ cups cashews

1 cup sliced mushrooms

1 cup sliced celery

1 can (10¾ ounces) condensed cream of mushroom soup, undiluted

¼ cup chopped green onion

2 tablespoons butter

1½ tablespoons soy sauce

Hot cooked rice

1. Combine chicken, cashews, mushrooms, celery, soup, green onion, butter and soy sauce in **CROCK-POT®** slow cooker.

2. Cover; cook on LOW 6 to 8 hours or on HIGH 4 to 6 hours or until done. Serve over rice.

Note: *Time spent in the kitchen cooking with your kids is time well spent. You can share the value of preparing wholesome, comforting, nurturing foods while equipping them with the skills to create their own food traditions in the future. Even young children can participate in family meal preparation. Just remember these basics: Always make sure children are well-supervised in the kitchen. Only adults should use sharp utensils, plug in or turn on electric appliances or handle hot foods. Be sure to only assign tasks that the child can do and feel good about.*

Makes 6 servings

CROCK·POT
· THE ORIGINAL SLOW COOKER ·

WEEKNIGHT WINNERS

Spanish Paella with Chicken and Sausage

1 tablespoon olive oil

2 pounds chicken thighs

1 medium onion, chopped

1 clove garlic, minced

1 pound hot smoked sausages, sliced

1 can (14½ ounces) stewed tomatoes

1 cup Arborio rice

4 cups chicken broth

1 pinch saffron (optional)

½ cup frozen peas, thawed

1. Heat oil in large skillet over medium-high heat. Brown chicken on all sides and place in **CROCK-POT®**slow cooker.

2. Add onion to skillet, cook and stir until translucent. Stir in garlic, sausages, tomatoes, rice, chicken broth and saffron, if desired. Pour mixture over chicken.

3. Cover and cook on HIGH 3 to 4 hours or until chicken and rice are tender. Remove chicken pieces to platter and fluff rice with fork. Stir in peas. Spoon rice onto platter with chicken.

Makes 4 servings

Greek Chicken Pitas with Creamy Mustard Sauce

Filling

- 1 **medium green bell pepper, cored, seeded and sliced into ½-inch strips**
- 1 **medium onion, cut into 8 wedges**
- 1 **pound boneless skinless chicken breasts, rinsed and patted dry**
- 1 **tablespoon extra-virgin olive oil**
- 2 **teaspoons dried Greek seasoning blend**
- ¼ **teaspoon salt**

Sauce

- ¼ **cup plain fat-free yogurt**
- ¼ **cup mayonnaise**
- 1 **tablespoon prepared mustard**
- ¼ **teaspoon salt**
- 4 **whole pita rounds**
- ½ **cup crumbled feta cheese**

   Optional toppings: sliced cucumbers, sliced tomatoes, kalamata olives

1. Coat **CROCK-POT®** slow cooker with nonstick cooking spray. Place bell pepper and onion in bottom. Add chicken, and drizzle on oil. Sprinkle evenly with seasoning and ¼ teaspoon salt. Cover; cook on HIGH 1¾ hours or until chicken is no longer pink and vegetables are crisp-tender.

2. Remove chicken and slice. Remove vegetables using slotted spoon.

3. To prepare sauce: Combine yogurt, mayonnaise, mustard and ¼ teaspoon salt in small bowl. Whisk until smooth.

4. Warm pitas according to package directions. Cut in half, and fill with chicken, sauce, vegetables and feta cheese. Top as desired.

Makes 4 servings

Roast Chicken with Peas, Prosciutto and Cream

1 cut-up whole chicken (about 2½ pounds)

   Salt and black pepper, to taste

5 ounces prosciutto, diced

1 small white onion, finely chopped

½ cup dry white wine

1 package (10 ounces) frozen peas

½ cup heavy cream

1½ tablespoons cornstarch

2 tablespoons water

4 cups farfalle pasta, cooked al dente

1. Season chicken pieces with salt and pepper. Combine chicken, prosciutto, onion and wine in **CROCK-POT®** slow cooker. Cover; cook on HIGH 3½ to 4 hours or on LOW 8 to 10 hours, until chicken is no longer pink in center.

2. During last 30 minutes of cooking, add frozen peas and heavy cream to cooking liquid.

3. Remove chicken with slotted spoon. Carve meat and set aside on warmed platter.

4. Combine cornstarch and water. Add to cooking liquid in **CROCK-POT®** slow cooker. Cover; cook on HIGH 10 to 15 minutes or until thickened.

5. To serve, spoon pasta onto individual plates. Place chicken on pasta and top each portion with sauce.

Makes 6 servings

70

Chicken and Ham with Biscuits

2 cans (10¾ ounces each) condensed cream of mushroom soup, undiluted

2 cups diced ham

2 cups diced boneless chicken

1 package (12 ounces) frozen peas and onions

1 package (8 ounces) frozen corn

½ cup chopped celery

¼ teaspoon dried marjoram

¼ teaspoon dried thyme

2 tablespoons cornstarch

2 teaspoons water

1 to 2 cans refrigerated buttermilk biscuits

4 tablespoons (½ stick) butter, melted

1. Combine soup, ham, chicken, frozen vegetables, celery, marjoram and thyme in **CROCK-POT®** slow cooker. Cover; cook on LOW 4 to 5 hours or on HIGH 1 to 3 hours.

2. Mix cornstarch and water together in bowl. Stir into **CROCK-POT®** slow cooker. Cook 10 to 15 minutes longer or until mixture has thickened.

3. Meanwhile, place biscuits on baking sheet and brush with butter. Bake according to package directions until biscuits are golden brown.

4. To serve, ladle stew into bowls and top with warm biscuit.

Makes 8 to 10 servings

Braised Italian Chicken with Tomatoes and Olives

2 pounds boneless skinless chicken thighs

1 teaspoon kosher salt

½ teaspoon black pepper

½ cup all-purpose flour

Olive oil

1 can (14½ ounces) diced tomatoes, drained

⅓ cup dry red wine

⅓ cup pitted quartered kalamata olives

1 clove garlic, minced

1 teaspoon chopped fresh rosemary

½ teaspoon crushed red pepper flakes

Cooked linguini or spaghetti

Grated or shredded Parmesan cheese (optional)

1. Season chicken with salt and pepper. Spread flour on plate, and lightly dredge chicken in flour, coating both sides.

2. Heat oil in skillet over medium heat until hot. Sear chicken in 2 or 3 batches until well browned on both sides. Use additional oil as needed to prevent sticking. Transfer to **CROCK-POT®** slow cooker.

3. Add tomatoes, wine, olives and garlic. Cover; cook on LOW 4 to 5 hours.

4. Add rosemary and red pepper flakes; stir in. Cover; cook on LOW 1 hour longer. Serve over linguini. Garnish with cheese, if desired.

Makes 4 servings

Chicken and Spicy Black Bean Tacos

1 can (15 ounces) black beans, drained and rinsed

1 can (10 ounces) tomatoes with mild green chiles, drained

1½ teaspoons chili powder

¾ teaspoon ground cumin

1 tablespoon plus 1 teaspoon extra-virgin olive oil, divided

12 ounces boneless skinless chicken breasts, rinsed and patted dry

12 crisp corn taco shells

Optional toppings: shredded lettuce, diced tomatoes, shredded cheese, sour cream, ripe olives

1. Coat **CROCK-POT®** slow cooker with nonstick cooking spray. Add beans and tomatoes with chiles. Blend chili powder and cumin with 1 teaspoon oil and rub onto chicken breasts. Place chicken in **CROCK-POT®** slow cooker. Cover; cook on HIGH 1¾ hours.

2. Remove chicken and slice. Transfer bean mixture to bowl using slotted spoon. Stir in 1 tablespoon oil.

3. To serve, warm taco shells according to package directions. Fill with equal amounts of bean mixture and chicken. Add toppings as desired.

Makes 4 servings

Chicken Cacciatore

¼ cup vegetable oil

2½ to 3 pounds chicken tenders, cut into bite-size pieces

1 can (28 ounces) crushed Italian-style tomatoes

2 cans (8 ounces each) Italian-style tomato sauce

1 medium onion, chopped

1 can (4 ounces) sliced mushrooms, drained

2 cloves garlic, minced

1 teaspoon salt

1 teaspoon dried oregano leaves

½ teaspoon dried thyme leaves

½ teaspoon black pepper

Hot cooked spaghetti or rice

1. Heat oil in large skillet over medium-low heat. Brown chicken on all sides. Drain excess fat.

2. Transfer chicken to **CROCK-POT®** slow cooker. Add remaining ingredients except spaghetti. Cover; cook on LOW 6 to 8 hours. Serve over spaghetti.

Makes 6 to 8 servings

Chicken and Mushroom Fettuccine Alfredo

1½ **pounds chicken breast cutlets, rinsed, patted dry and cut into strips**

2 **packages (8 ounces each) cremini mushrooms, cut into thirds**

½ **teaspoon salt**

½ **teaspoon black pepper**

¼ **teaspoon garlic powder**

2 **packages (8 ounces each) cream cheese, cut into pieces**

2 **sticks butter, cut into pieces**

1½ **cups grated Parmesan cheese, plus additional for serving**

1½ **cups whole milk**

1 **box (8 ounces) fettucine noodles**

1. Spray **CROCK-POT®** slow cooker with nonstick cooking spray. Add chicken strips in single layer. Distribute mushrooms evenly over chicken. Sprinkle salt, pepper and garlic powder over mushrooms.

2. In medium saucepan over medium heat, stir together cream cheese, butter, cheese and milk. Whisk continuously until smooth and heated through. Pour mixture over mushrooms, pushing down any mushrooms that float to top. Cover and cook on LOW 4 to 5 hours.

3. Cook fettuccine according to package directions. Drain. Add fettuccine to **CROCK-POT®** slow cooker and toss gently with sauce. Serve with Parmesan cheese.

Makes 6 to 8 servings

INDEX

Angel Wings 8

Asian Barbecue Skewers...................... 4

Asian Chicken "Fondue" 15

Autumn Chicken 58

Basque Chicken with Peppers.......... 48

Bistro Chicken in Rich Cream
Sauce 40

Black and White Chili..................... 18

Braised Italian Chicken with
Tomatoes and Olives.................... 73

Cashew Chicken 64

Cerveza Chicken Enchilada
Casserole...................................... 52

Chicken and Asiago Stuffed
Mushrooms..................................... 9

Chicken and Black Bean Chili......... 32

Chicken and Chile Pepper Stew...... 28

Chicken and Ham with Biscuits...... 72

Chicken and Mushroom
Fettuccine Alfredo........................ 78

Chicken & Rice................................. 58

Chicken and Spicy Black
Bean Tacos 74

Chicken and Sweet Potato Stew...... 31

Chicken and Vegetable Chowder 30

Chicken Cacciatore 76

Chicken Croustade 6

Chicken in Honey Sauce.................. 60

Chicken Liver Pâté 10

Chicken Parmesan with Eggplant ... 46

Chicken Stew with
Herb Dumplings.......................... 23

Chicken Tangier............................... 34

Chicken Teriyaki.............................. 60

Chinese Chicken Stew 20

Chipotle Chicken Casserole 57

Chipotle Chicken Stew 24

Coq au Vin....................................... 44

Cranberry-Barbecue
Chicken Wings 14

Dijon Chicken Thighs
with Artichoke Sauce 56

Forty-Clove Chicken........................ 38

Greek Chicken and Orzo 47

Greek Chicken Pitas with
Creamy Mustard Sauce 68

Greek-Style Chicken Stew............... 22

Honey-Glazed Chicken Wings.......... 8

Indian-Style Apricot Chicken.......... 42

Mediterranean Chicken Breasts
and Wild Rice 54

Moroccan Spiced Chicken Wings ... 12

Oriental Chicken Wings 12

Provençal Lemon and Olive
Chicken 62

Quatro Frijoles con Pollo Cantaro ...26

Roast Chicken with Peas,
Prosciutto and Cream 70

Spanish Paella with Chicken
and Sausage 66

Stuffed Baby Bell Peppers.................. 2

Stuffed Chicken Breasts 36

Thai Chicken 50

Thai Coconut Chicken Meatballs.... 16